D0745854

How Do Things Move?

Pushing and Pulling

Sue Barraclough

Raintree

Chicago, Illinois

Customer Service   888–454–2279

Visit our website at www.heinemannlibrary.com

Photo research by Ruth Blair, Erica Newbery, and Kay Altwegg
Designed by Jo Hinton-Malivoire and bigtop design ltd
Printed and bound in China by South China Printing Company
10 09 08 07 06
10 9 8 7 6 5 4 3 2 1

Library of Congress Cataloging-in-Publication Data
Barraclough, Sue.
  Pushing and pulling / Sue Barraclough.
     p. cm. -- (How do things move?)
  Includes bibliographical references and index.
  ISBN 1-4109-2258-8 (library binding-hardcover) -- ISBN 1-4109-2263-4 (pbk.)
 1. Force and energy--Juvenile literature. 2. Power (Mechanics)--Juvenile literature. I. Title.
II. Series.
  QC73.4.B379 2005
  531'.6--dc22
                                    2005029846

Acknowledgments
The author and publisher are grateful to the following for permission to reproduce copyright
material: Alamy pp. **10, 23 bottom right** (Index Stock), **11, 23 top left** (A Room with
Views), **12** (Iain Davidson Photographic), **15, 23 bottom left** (Sarkis Images); Corbis pp. **4,
5**; Corbis pp. **8, 9** (Ed Bock), **13, 22 top left** (LWA-Dann Tardif), **16, 17** (John Henley);
Getty Images p. **7**; Getty Images pp. **6, 22 bottom** (Reportage/Per-Anders Pettersson), **18,
19, 23 top right** (Photonica), **21, 22 top right** (photodisc); Harcourt Education pp. **14,
20** (Tudor Photography).

Cover photograph reproduced with permission of Getty (Peter Cade).

Every effort has been made to contact copyright holders of any material reproduced in this
book. Any omissions will be rectified in subsequent printings if notice is given to the
publisher.

Some words are shown in bold, **like this**. You can find out
what they mean by looking in the glossary.

Contents

Pushing and Pulling

push

You can push things to make them move.

pull

You can pull things to make them move.

Pushing

A push can make a toy car move.

A hard push can make
something move faster.

Pulling

You pull a **wagon** to move it.

Why is this wagon hard to pull?

Swinging and Spinning

A push can make a
swing go higher.

A push can make a merry-go-round spin.

Moving Up

You push yourself up on a seesaw.

You pull yourself up
on monkey bars.

Moving Along

Is this girl pushing
or pulling?

Is this boy pushing
or pulling?

Tug-of-War

Each team is pulling hard on the rope.

Which team do you
think is pulling harder?

Arm Wrestling

Both children are
pushing hard.

Who do you think
is pushing harder?

Light and Heavy

The toy car is light.
Is it hard to push?

The **wagon** is heavy.
Is it hard to pull?

Push or Pull?

Can you remember which things you push and which things you pull?

23

Glossary

merry-go-round playground ride that spins in a circle

wagon cart with four wheels that is used to move things

Index

Notes for Adults

The *How Do Things Move?* series provides young children with a first opportunity to learn about motion. Each book encourages children to notice and ask questions about the types of movement they see around them.

These books will also help children extend their vocabulary, as they will hear some new words. Since words are used in context in the book this should enable young children to gradually incorporate them into their own vocabulary.

Follow-up activities
- Show your child two inanimate objects, one heavy and one light. Ask them to decide which item would be easier to push, then get them to test their theory by pushing both objects.
- Attach a toy car to a piece of string and then pull it along at first slowly and then fast. Ask your child if they can identify what made the car move slowly and what made it move fast. Then get them to try for themselves.